THE BEST 50
SALSAS

Christie and Thomas Katona

D0094397

BRISTOL PUBLISHING ENTERPRISES
San Leandro, California

Printed in the United States of America.

ISBN 1-55867-112-9

Cover design: Frank Paredes
Cover photography: John Benson
Food stylist: Suzanne Carreiro

TIPS FOR MAKING AND SERVING SALSAS

Salsas are the newest culinary rage. For the first time in history, salsas are outselling ketchup at the grocery store and people everywhere are whipping up their own renditions at home. Salsas are easy to prepare and the ingredients vary from common to unusual. The only tool necessary is a sharp knife or a food processor.

A salsa is a spicy sauce made with vegetables or fruits. Although the traditional salsa is made with tomatoes, onions and peppers, people have discovered that other vegetables can be used to make delicious salsas, and spicy fruit salsas are wonderful accompaniments to many dishes. Cooks can be as innovative as they wish, experimenting with different fresh or dried chiles, exotic fruits, fresh tomatillos or various kinds of avocados.

Salsas are also low in fat and calories while adding a great

amount of flavor to your food.

Most salsas keep well in the refrigerator for a few days. Their flavors are enhanced by serving them at room temperature, so plan on removing them from the refrigerator an hour or so before serving.

SOME FAVORITE WAYS TO ENJOY SALSAS

- with any and all Mexican food
- on baked potatoes
- as a topping for rice
- in meat loaf or stuffed peppers
- as a topping for pizza
- in soups or stews
- over a brick of cream cheese as an appetizer with crackers
- in burgers or sandwiches

- combined with sour cream or unflavored yogurt as a dip for chips
- as a topping for cheese soufflés or frittatas
- as a sauce for grilled poultry, fish, seafood, pork or other meat
- in grilled cheese sandwiches
- on scrambled eggs or omelets
- as a topping for cheese and garlic grits or polenta
- on hot dogs
- with seviche
- stirred into cheese sauce as a "fondue" for tortilla chips
- on cottage cheese

SOME INGREDIENTS FOR SALSAS

avocado - a native fruit of America that is high in vitamins and adds a delicious buttery richness. Avocados darken when exposed to air, so brush them with lemon juice or add just at the last minute. The dark, pebbly-skinned Hass avocado has the best flavor.

cilantro - the fresh, young, leafy plantlets of the herb coriander. Cilantro packs a flavor wallop. It is used in salads and various dishes as a flavoring and garnish and is sometimes called Chinese parsley. Chop the leaves along with the stems to add wonderful flavor to salsas.

chile peppers - there are more than 140 varieties of chiles grown in Mexico. Many are fiery hot and others are sweet and mild. The hotness of the chile is in the ribs or veins, and the seeds are hot due to their proximity to the veins. When the chile is cut in half, yellow or orange veins are an indication that the chile will be a

potent one. The oil in the chile, *capsaisin*, can cause severe burns, so never touch your face or eyes when handling hot chiles. Some people with sensitive skin wear rubber gloves. It also helps to handle chiles under running water. A small, sharp knife or serrated grapefruit spoon works well to remove ribs, veins and seeds from chiles. If by chance you eat a chile that's far too hot for your comfort, milk is a great soother.

» **anaheim** - a long (4 to 7 inches), light green chile with a mild flavor. They are sold fresh or in cans, whole or diced.

» **ancho** - the most widely used dried chile in Mexico. It is reddish brown in color and very wrinkled. It is mild and sweet in flavor.

» **arbol** - a small dried red chile, with the smallest being the hottest.

» **bell pepper** - the most frequently used pepper in the United States. Most familiar in green and red, they are also avail-

able in deep dark purple, yellow and orange. Their sweet, mild flavor and crisp, firm texture make them a favorite for snacks, salads, stir-fry, pizza and Mexican dishes.

» **caribe** - a crushed, dried red chile, often seen in pizza parlors. The flavor improves when heated.

» **cascabel** - a round, rust-brown chile, about 1½ to 2 inches in diameter. It has a nutty, sweet flavor and loose seeds. It is often available dried.

» **chipotle** - often sold canned as "chipotle en adobo." It is used as a condiment, much like Tabasco.

» **fresno** - about 2 inches long and 1 inch in diameter, these bright green chiles change in color to orange and red when fully mature. They are often canned or bottled and labeled as "hot chile peppers."

» **habañero** - the hottest chile of all, one thousand times hotter than a jalapeño. Used in Carribean cuisine where it is re-

ferred to as a "Scotch bonnet." Due to its extreme heat, it is not readily available.

» **jalapeño** - the most popular hot chile in the United States. Sold fresh in most produce sections at the local grocery store, jalapeños are dark green in color and 2 to 3 inches in length. They are also sold pickled and sliced.

» **pasilla** - can be as long as 12 inches and 1 inch in diameter. They are dark green and turn to dark brown as they mature. Often dried, this chile is particularly good in salsas for fish and in moles.

» **pimiento** - available canned in the United States, these chiles are heart-shaped, softer and sweeter than the common red bell pepper.

» **poblano** - mild to fairly pungent, wedge-shaped, dark green pepper with a thick, leathery skin. This chile is highly regarded for its flavor complexity.

» **serrano** - slightly smaller than jalapeños (1½ to 3 inches long), this light green chile is very hot but has excellent flavor. Remove the stems and seeds inside to reduce the heat.

tomatillo - related to the gooseberry family, tomatillos are sold fresh and in cans. They are light green in color with a papery brown husk. Remove the husk and rinse the tomatillo thoroughly before using. They have a tart flavor and are used both fresh and cooked.

WATERMELON AND AVOCADO SALSA

Prepare this salsa at the last moment. The watermelon becomes too juicy if it is held longer than an hour. This is very tasty with teriyaki chicken.

1 cup diced watermelon
1 avocado, peeled, seeded and diced
¼ cup diced red onion
2 tbs. chopped fresh cilantro
grated zest (colored peel without
white membrane) and juice of 1 lime

Gently combine all ingredients. Serve immediately.

Makes 1½ cups

THREE BERRY SALSA

Serve this salsa on a bed of bright green spinach leaves topped with grilled chicken breast for a colorful presentation. Try it with chips or Jack cheese quesadillas.

1 cup blueberries
1 cup stemmed, quartered
  strawberries
1 cup raspberries
1 cup diced tomatoes
1/4 cup chopped red onion
1/4 cup chopped fresh cilantro

grated zest (colored peel without white membrane) and
  juice of 1 orange
grated zest and juice of 1 lime
2 tsp. sugar
1/2 tsp. salt

Combine all ingredients. Cover and chill.

Makes 4 cups

ORANGE GINGER SALSA

Store ginger root in vodka in a jar in your refrigerator and it will last until you've used it all. Ginger root also can be frozen. It adds a wonderful fresh tang to many foods.

2 cups diced fresh oranges, peeled, seeded, membrane removed
1 cup seeded, diced plum tomatoes
½ cup diced red onion
2 tsp. finely minced ginger root

2 tbs. fresh lime juice
2 tbs. olive oil
2 tbs. finely chopped fresh cilantro
1 tsp. salt
1 tsp. sugar
½ tsp. ground coriander

Combine all ingredients. Cover and chill.

Makes 3 cups

MIXED FRUIT SALSA

Eliminate the jalapeño and red onion, and you can serve this on frozen yogurt for a fresh and delicious dessert. In its spicy state, it is wonderful with grilled fish.

2 bananas, peeled and diced into ½-inch pieces
½ cup diced fresh or frozen peaches (½-inch pieces)
½ cup fresh or frozen raspberries
2 kiwis, peeled and diced into ½-inch pieces
½ cup stemmed diced fresh strawberries (½-inch pieces)
1 jalapeño chile, minced
¼ cup minced red onion
sugar or Equal to taste
1 tbs. tequila

Gently stir all ingredients together. Cover and chill.

Makes 2 cups

PINEAPPLE AND DATE SALSA

This is excellent on a turkey sandwich with cream cheese. Try it with poultry or pork.

1 cup finely diced fresh pineapple
1/2 cup chopped fresh cranberries
1/3 cup chopped dried dates
1/4 cup finely chopped red onion
1 tbs. honey
1 tsp. lemon juice
1 tsp. finely minced ginger root
1/4 tsp. cayenne pepper

Combine all ingredients. Cover and chill.

Makes 2 cups

SUMMER SALSA

Serve this colorful, tasty salsa with roasted Cornish game hens or grilled chicken for a change of pace.

2 cups diced strawberries
½ cup chopped red onion
½ cup chopped fresh cilantro
1 jalapeño chile, finely chopped
¼ cup finely chopped fresh mint
2 tbs. olive oil
¼ cup balsamic vinegar
salt and white pepper

Combine all ingredients. Cover and chill.

Makes 2½ cups

PEAR SALSA

This makes a nice accompaniment to pork or chicken.

2 pears, peeled, cored and diced
2 dried pear halves, finely chopped
1/4 cup chopped red onion
1/4 cup chopped fresh cilantro
grated zest (colored peel without white membrane) and
juice of 1 lime
1 tbs. minced ginger root
1 jalapeño chile, seeded and minced
1/2 tsp. salt
1/4 tsp. crushed red pepper flakes

Combine all ingredients. Cover and chill.

Makes 2 1/2 cups

CRANBERRY SALSA

Cranberries are always a good accompaniment to poultry. This salsa is good on turkey sandwiches, and gives a delicious flavor burst to Brie quesadillas.

1½ cups fresh or frozen cranberries
⅓ cup sugar
¼ cup thinly sliced green onions
¼ cup chopped fresh cilantro
grated zest (colored peel without white membrane) and
juice of 1 lime
1 jalapeño chile, seeded and minced
2 tsp. finely chopped ginger root
¼ tsp. salt

Coarsely chop cranberries. Combine with remaining ingredients, cover and chill. Or, coarsely chop all ingredients in a food processor, cover and chill.

Makes 1½ cups

GRAPE SALSA

This salsa is unusual and colorful. Serve it with grilled chicken.

2 cups halved seedless red
  grapes
1/4 cup diced red onion
1 jalapeño chile, seeded
  and minced
2 tbs. chopped fresh cilantro
1 clove garlic, minced

1 tbs. lemon juice
1 tbs. rice vinegar
1/4 cup slivered almonds,
  lightly toasted
1/2 tsp. salt
dash cayenne pepper

Combine all ingredients. Cover and chill.

Makes 2½ cups

PEACH AND GINGER SALSA

This is a favorite with grilled lamb chops.

2 cups peeled, diced peaches
½ cup chopped red bell pepper
½ cup chopped red onion
1 serrano chile, minced
¼ cup chopped fresh mint
1½ tbs. lime juice
2 tsp. grated ginger root
2 tsp. olive oil
salt

Combine ingredients and chill for 30 minutes.

Makes 3 cups

MELON, CUCUMBER AND MINT SALSA

This very refreshing salsa is delicious with grilled fish.

2 cups diced honeydew melon
2 tomatoes, seeded and diced
1/2 cup peeled, seeded, diced
  cucumber
2 tbs. red wine vinegar
1 tbs. vegetable oil

1 tbs. chopped fresh parsley
2 tsp. thinly sliced fresh chives
2 tsp. chopped fresh mint
2 tsp. sugar
1 tsp. salt
1/2 tsp. white pepper

Combine all ingredients. Cover and chill.

Makes 4 cups

PAPAYA AND WATERMELON SALSA

This is another salsa that does not keep well because the watermelon is so juicy. Be sure to prepare it just before serving.

1 cup peeled, seeded, diced papaya
1/2 cup seeded, diced watermelon (1/2-inch pieces)
1/4 cup peeled, seeded, diced cucumber
1/4 cup diced red onion
grated zest (colored peel without white membrane) and
juice of 1 lime
2 tbs. chopped fresh cilantro
2 tsp. olive oil
1 tsp. minced jalapeño chile
salt and pepper

Combine all ingredients. Cover and chill.

Makes 2 cups

PINEAPPLE AND MANGO SALSA

Fresh fruit salsa is delicious with grilled chicken, and goes well with grilled fish, too. Use Thai fish sauce if you can find it, or substitute soy sauce.

1 cup diced fresh pineapple
1 cup peeled, diced fresh mango
1 cup diced tomatoes
1/4 cup thinly sliced green onions
2 tbs. vegetable oil
1 tbs. chopped fresh cilantro
1 tbs. soy sauce

1 tbs. fish sauce
2 tsp. finely minced ginger root
1 jalapeño chile, finely chopped
2 tsp. rice vinegar
1 tsp. minced garlic
1 tsp. honey

Combine all ingredients. Cover and chill.

Makes 3 cups

CANTALOUPE LIME SALSA

Try this with grilled fish such as halibut or swordfish. It's also delightful with grilled prawns.

1 cup diced cantaloupe
1/4 cup chopped red onion
1 tbs. diced green chiles, optional
2 tbs. chopped fresh cilantro
grated zest (colored peel without white membrane)
and juice of 1 lime
1/2 tsp. white pepper

Combine all ingredients. Cover and chill.

Makes 1 1/2 cups

SPICY TROPICAL SALSA

This fruity, spicy salsa is excellent with grilled fish or chicken.

1 cup diced mango
1 cup diced papaya
1 cup diced pineapple
2 kiwis, peeled and diced
1 tsp. crushed red pepper flakes
¼ cup seasoned rice wine vinegar
3 tbs. chopped fresh cilantro

Combine all ingredients. Cover and chill.

Makes 4 cups

TANGERINE SALSA

Refreshing and colorful with citrus tang, this salsa could also be prepared with fresh oranges. It is excellent with firm-textured fish such as halibut, sturgeon or swordfish.

4 tangerines, peeled, membrane and seeds removed,
sectioned
4 plum tomatoes, seeded and diced
1/3 cup diced red onion
1/3 cup diced red bell pepper
1/4 cup diced poblano chile
1 tbs. fresh lime juice
1 tbs. peanut oil, or other light oil

1 tsp. ground coriander
½ tsp. pepper
¼ tsp. salt
2 tbs. chopped fresh cilantro

Combine all ingredients. Cover and chill.

Makes 2 cups

MANGO AND SUN-DRIED TOMATO SALSA

Sun-dried tomatoes originally come from Italy and Americans have fallen in love with their intense flavor and interesting, chewy texture. You'll find them packaged dry or packed in jars in herb-infused oil.

1 ripe mango, peeled and diced
1/4 cup chopped sun-dried tomatoes
1/4 cup chopped red onion
1/4 cup chopped green onions
2 tbs. minced fresh cilantro leaves
1 jalapeño chile, seeded and minced
2 tbs. olive oil
2 tbs. fresh lime juice
1/4 tsp. salt

Combine all ingredients. Cover and chill.

Makes 2 cups

GRAPEFRUIT SALSA

Here's another salsa that's great with grilled fish. To seed and devein fresh chiles, cut them in half lengthwise and remove veins and seeds with a small sharp knife or a serrated grapefruit spoon.

6 pink grapefruits, peeled, membrane removed, chopped
4 serrano chiles, diced
1/4 cup chopped red onion
1/4 cup chopped fresh cilantro
1/4 tsp. salt

Combine all ingredients. Cover and chill.

Makes 2 cups

ORANGE AND BLACK BEAN SALSA

This salsa makes an excellent vegetarian meal spooned over rice. Top with shredded Jack or cheddar cheese if you like.

1 can (15 oz.) black beans, rinsed and drained
2 oranges, peeled and diced
1 jalapeño chile, seeded and finely chopped
1/4 cup chopped fresh cilantro
1/4 cup chopped green onions
3 tsp. oil
1 tsp. lemon juice
1/4 tsp. salt
1/4 tsp. ground cumin

Combine all ingredients. Cover and chill.

Makes 2 cups

MANGO AND TANGERINE SALSA

People with sensitive skin should wear rubber gloves when peeling chiles and hold them under cool running water. <u>Never</u> touch your eyes when handling chiles!

1 mango, peeled and chopped
2 tangerines, peeled and chopped
¼ cup diced red bell pepper
¼ cup sliced green onions
1 jalapeño chile, seeded and finely chopped
2 tsp. orange juice
¼ tsp. ground coriander
¼ tsp. salt

Combine all ingredients. Cover and chill.

Makes 1 cup

MANGO AND CORN SALSA

Fresh mangoes are becoming a popular item in the produce stand. Select a mango that is just beginning to yield to pressure. Mangoes can be stored at room temperature to ripen.

1 mango, peeled and diced
1/2 cup whole kernel corn
1/2 cup diced green bell pepper
1/4 cup diced red onion
2 tbs. chopped fresh cilantro
1 tsp. lime juice
1 tsp. vegetable oil
1/4 tsp. salt

Combine all ingredients. Cover and chill.

Makes 1 1/2 cups

MIXED FRUIT SALSA WITH GINGER

Frozen peach slices are almost indistinguishable from fresh in the off season, and are easy to keep on hand.

1 peach, peeled and chopped
1 cup diced honeydew melon
1 cup halved red flame grapes
2 tbs. chopped fresh cilantro
2 green onions, chopped
1/2 tsp. crushed red pepper flakes
1 tsp. grated ginger root
1 tsp. honey
dash salt

Combine all ingredients. Cover and chill.

Makes 2 1/2 cups

RASPBERRY SALSA

Try this with Cornish game hens or roast duck. To use frozen berries, thaw and drain off as much juice or syrup as possible.

2 cups fresh raspberries
2 jalapeño chiles, seeded and finely chopped
1/4 cup chopped red onion
2 tbs. minced fresh cilantro
2 tbs. raspberry vinegar
1/4 tsp. salt

Gently stir ingredients together. Cover and chill for 30 minutes to blend flavors.

Makes 2 cups

PINEAPPLE SALSA

Crushed pineapple packed in its own juice can also be used in this recipe. It's great on soft chicken tacos.

2 cups diced fresh pineapple
4 kiwis, peeled and diced
¼ cup chopped red onion
2 jalapeño chiles, seeded and finely chopped
2 tbs. chopped fresh cilantro
1 tbs. lime juice
¼ tsp. salt

Combine all ingredients. Cover and chill.

Makes 2½ cups

PEACH SALSA

*Cover a brick of cream cheese with **Peach Salsa** and serve it with crackers as an appetizer. You can use this idea with almost any salsa.*

1½ cups chopped peeled peaches
¾ cup chopped red bell pepper
¾ cup seeded chopped cucumber
¼ cup sliced green onion
2 jalapeño chiles, seeded and finely chopped
2 tbs. honey
2 tbs. lime juice
1 tbs. chopped fresh cilantro

Combine all ingredients. Cover and chill.

Makes 2½ cups

APRICOT SALSA

Stir a cup of this salsa into sour cream or unflavored yogurt and use it as a sauce with pork or chicken.

1½ cups chopped fresh apricots
¾ cup chopped green bell pepper
1¾ cups seeded chopped cucumber
¼ cup sliced green onion
1 jalapeño chile, seeded and finely chopped
2 tbs. honey
2 tbs. lime juice
1 tbs. finely chopped fresh cilantro

Combine all ingredients. Cover and chill.

Makes 2½ cups

PINEAPPLE AND PAPAYA SALSA

A papaya is a tropical fruit with orange pulp and yellow rind when ripe. You can eat it like melon or bake it and serve it as a side dish. Slices of papaya are wonderful on a fruit platter or grilled and brushed with curry or ginger butter. If you haven't done so already, try it! It will become one of your favorites.

2 cups finely diced fresh pineapple
1 cup finely diced fresh papaya
½ cup finely diced red bell pepper
½ cup finely diced sweet onion
1 clove garlic, minced
1 serrano chile, seeded and finely minced
2 tbs. snipped fresh mint leaves

Combine all ingredients. Cover and chill overnight.

Makes 3 cups

PEPPER AND PAPAYA SALSA

Be sure to wear rubber gloves when you seed and chop the poblano chile.

3 cups peeled, seeded, diced papaya
1/2 cup finely chopped red bell pepper
1/2 cup finely chopped green bell pepper
1/2 cup finely chopped fresh pineapple
1/4 cup finely chopped red onion
1/4 cup finely chopped fresh cilantro
1/2 fresh poblano chile, seeded and finely chopped
2 tbs. lime juice
1 tbs. lemon juice

Combine all ingredients. Cover and chill.

Makes 4 cups

KIWI SALSA

If you can't find fresh tomatillos, they are available canned in the Mexican foods section of your grocery store. Fresh kiwi will keep for weeks in the refrigerator.

1 cup peeled chopped kiwis (about 5-6)
⅓ cup sliced green onions
⅓ cup chopped tomatillos
1 jalapeño chile, seeded and minced
2 tbs. chopped fresh cilantro
¼ cup rice wine vinegar
1 tbs. unsweetened pineapple juice
1 tsp. sugar

Combine all ingredients. Cover and chill.

Makes 2 cups

BING CHERRY SALSA

This salsa should be served immediately. Try it with pork, chicken or on top of cream cheese.

1 cup pitted fresh Bing cherries
1 tbs. minced green bell pepper
2 tbs. chopped fresh basil
grated zest (colored peel without white
membrane) and juice of 1 lemon
$1/4$ tsp. Worcestershire sauce
dash Tabasco Sauce
salt

Chop ingredients to medium coarseness and combine. Season to taste and serve immediately.

Makes 1 cup

FREEZER SALSA

When your garden is overflowing with tomatoes, make some of this delicious salsa for the freezer. Most salsas don't freeze well, but this one was created for the freezer.

7 lb. fresh tomatoes
3 cups seeded, chopped chile peppers, such as
anaheim or poblano
1/2 cup seeded, finely chopped jalapeño or serrano chiles
2 cups chopped onion
5 cloves garlic, minced
1/2 cup chopped fresh cilantro
1/2 cup vinegar
1 tbs. sugar
1 tsp. salt
1 tsp. pepper

Peel, seed and coarsely chop tomatoes. Place tomatoes in a large colander and drain for 30 minutes. Place drained tomatoes in a large kettle and bring to a boil. Reduce heat and simmer, uncovered, for 45 minutes or until thickened. Add remaining ingredients and bring to a boil. Remove from heat and place kettle in a sink filled with ice water to cool quickly. When cool, spoon into freezer-proof containers, leaving ½ inch head space. Freeze for up to 6 months.

Makes 4 pints

GARBANZO SALSA

This hearty salsa is excellent with Mexican food. It's great on cheddar cheese omelets for Sunday brunch. Serve with chorizo sausage, fresh fruit and corn muffins to round out your menu.

1 can (19 oz.) garbanzo beans, drained and pureed
3 cups chopped celery
1 can (28 oz.) peeled tomatoes, with juice
1 cucumber, peeled, seeded and diced
1 cup chopped fresh cilantro
1 can (4 oz.) chopped green chiles
½ cup sliced green onions
2 cloves garlic, minced
2 tbs. lemon juice
1 tbs. red wine vinegar

1 tbs. lime juice
1 tbs. crumbled dried oregano
1 tbs. Tabasco Sauce, or to taste
1 tsp. ground cumin
1 tsp. sugar

Combine ingredients in food processor. Process just to mix, leaving salsa chunky.

Makes 4 cups

ZUCCHINI SALSA

Just the thing to make when your garden is over-zealous with the zucchini crop.

10 cups finely chopped zucchini
3 cups finely chopped onion
3½ cups finely chopped anaheim chiles (about 25)
5 tbs. salt

Combine zucchini, onion, peppers and salt in a large bowl and refrigerate overnight. The next day, rinse thoroughly in a large colander. Squeeze dry in a large dish towel to remove excess moisture.

ADD:

5 cups chopped fresh
  tomatoes
2 cups cider vinegar
1 cup brown sugar
1 tbs. cornstarch
1 tbs. crushed red pepper
  flakes

1 tbs. ground cumin
2 tsp. dry mustard
1 tsp. pepper
1 tsp. turmeric
1 tsp. garlic powder
1 tsp. nutmeg

Combine ingredients until well mixed. Place in a large kettle (or 2!). Bring to a boil and reduce heat. Cook gently for 30 minutes. Pour into jars and refrigerate.

Makes 3 quarts

FRESH HERB SALSA

Use the ripest tomatoes available and serve at room temperature over freshly grilled tuna.

4 tomatoes, seeded and chopped
1/4 cup chopped fresh basil
2 tbs. chopped fresh marjoram
1 shallot, minced
2 tbs. balsamic vinegar
1 tbs. olive oil
salt and freshly ground pepper

Combine ingredients, cover and stand at room temperature 1 hour before serving.

Makes 1 1/2 cups

ARTICHOKE SALSA

Very tasty with grilled chicken. If you don't find fresh tomatillos, look for them in cans in the Mexican foods section of your supermarket.

6 tomatillos, husked and chopped
2 jars (4 oz. each) marinated artichokes, drained and chopped
1/4 cup sliced green onions
2 cloves garlic, minced
3 tbs. chopped fresh cilantro
grated zest (colored peel without white
membrane) and juice of 1 lime
1 jalapeño chile, seeded and finely chopped
1/2 tsp. salt

Combine all ingredients. Cover and chill.

Makes 2 cups

TOMATILLO APPLE SALSA

This spicy salsa is excellent with grilled salmon.

5 fresh tomatillos, husked and chopped
1 green bell pepper, seeded and chopped
1 red Delicious apple, cored and chopped
½ cup chopped red onion
3 tbs. chopped fresh cilantro
2 tbs. olive oil
1 tbs. fresh lemon juice
1 jalapeño chile, seeded and finely chopped
½ tsp. salt

Combine all ingredients. Cover and chill.

Makes 2 cups

HORSERADISH SALSA

This salsa has plenty of bite, and is particularly good with barbecued steak off the grill.

1 can (28 oz.) whole peeled tomatoes
1 can (4 oz.) diced green chiles
1 clove garlic, minced
½ cup chopped onion
1-3 tsp. drained bottled horseradish
few drops Tabasco Sauce
pepper

Drain tomatoes, discard liquid and chop coarsely. Add remaining ingredients, seasoning to taste.

Makes 2 cups

ROASTED CORN AND RED PEPPER SALSA

Plan on roasting the corn and peppers when you already have your grill going, the night before you intend to serve this salsa. This salsa has a particular affinity for pork. If you prefer, you may use commercially prepared roasted red bell peppers.

3 ears corn, shucked, silk removed
3 red bell peppers
1 tbs. vegetable oil
salt and pepper
¼ cup thinly sliced green onion
¼ cup chopped fresh cilantro
2 tsp. minced garlic
¼ cup fresh lemon juice

Grill corn and peppers until charred and tender, brushing with oil and sprinkling with salt and pepper. It will take about 5 minutes for the peppers and 10 for the corn. Turn frequently using tongs. Cool. Remove kernels from cob with a very sharp knife. Remove charred skin from peppers, halve, and remove ribs and seeds. Chop coarsely. Combine corn, peppers and remaining ingredients. Cover and chill.

Makes 2 cups

CORN AND BLACK BEAN SALSA

Try this salsa on refried beans, Mexican rice or as a topping for enchiladas. It's great on baked potatoes with sour cream and sliced green onions.

1 cup drained canned corn
1 cup canned black beans, rinsed
1 green bell pepper, seeded and diced
2 tomatoes, seeded and diced
1 avocado, seeded, peeled and diced

2 jalapeño chiles, seeded and finely diced
2 tbs. minced fresh cilantro
1/4 cup diced red onion
1 tbs. lime juice
1 tsp. ground cumin
1/4 tsp. salt

Combine all ingredients. Cover and chill.

Makes 3 cups

SWEET ONION SALSA

Sweet onions, such as Maui, Walla Walla, Texas Sweet 100's or Vidalia varieties, are gaining in popularity. Their availability is limited and because of their high liquid and sugar content, they do not keep well. Whenever you see them, be sure to get some to enjoy with burgers and sandwiches, in salads or in this tasty salsa.

1 cup chopped sweet onion
¾ cup chopped tomatoes
3 tbs. sliced ripe olives
1 can (4 oz.) chopped green
  chiles
2 tbs. chopped fresh cilantro

2 tbs. white wine vinegar
¼ tsp. salt
¼ tsp. pepper
¼ tsp. ground cumin
¼ tsp. Worcestershire sauce
¼ tsp. Tabasco Sauce

Combine all ingredients. Cover and chill.

Makes 2 cups

ROASTED TOMATILLO SALSA

Roasting the vegetables gives them a smoky depth of flavor that's hard to duplicate. This is a recipe to try when you have some spare time and want to impress your guests with authentic Mexican flavor.

¾ lb. tomatillos
¼ lb. small onions, about 1 inch with skins on
2 fresh anaheim chiles
½ cup chopped fresh cilantro
3 tbs. lime juice
1 tsp. salt

To roast tomatillos, remove paper husks. Set 1 tomatillo aside to add later. Place tomatillos, onions and chiles in a cast iron skillet or other very heavy skillet. Over high heat, roast vegetables, shaking the pan frequently to prevent burning. When vegetables are charred all over, about 15 minutes, remove from pan and cool. Peel onions. Remove charred skin from chiles, cut in half, and remove stems and seeds. Place all ingredients, including the 1 fresh tomatillo, in the work bowl of a food processor. Combine until coarsely chopped. Season to taste with lime juice and salt. Cover and chill for up to 4 days or serve immediately.

Makes 2 cups

TOMATO AND AVOCADO SALSA

Avocados are rich in vitamins and their creamy flavor is wonderful with spicy salsas. Several varieties are available, but the most flavorful is the pebbly dark-skinned Haas. To prevent avocados from turning black when exposed to air, sprinkle with lemon or lime juice. Wrap cut surfaces tightly with plastic wrap to seal.

3 cups chopped tomatoes
1 cup finely diced avocado
1/4 cup chopped red onion
1 jalapeño chile, seeded and
  minced

1/4 cup lime juice
1 tbs. chopped fresh cilantro
1 clove garlic, minced
1/4 tsp. salt

Combine all ingredients. Cover and chill.

Makes 4 cups

ROASTED GARLIC SALSA

Baking the garlic softens and mellows the flavor. Try this with blue corn nachos — sprinkle blue corn chips with cheddar and Monterey Jack cheeses. Top with sliced green onions, black olives, chopped tomatoes and pickled jalapeño slices. Wow!

3 large heads garlic
3 tbs. olive oil
2 cups chopped tomatoes
1/2 cup chopped onion

1 jalapeño chile, seeded and minced
2 tbs. chopped fresh cilantro
1 tsp. salt
1/2 tsp. Tabasco Sauce

Remove most of papery skin from garlic. Slice off tops, place in a shallow baking dish and drizzle with olive oil. Heat oven to 300° and roast garlic for 1 hour or until softened. Cool. Squeeze garlic cloves from skin and chop finely. Combine with remaining ingredients. Cover and chill.

Makes 2 cups

SALSA VERDE

This is an all-purpose green salsa. It's excellent with chicken enchiladas, grilled fish or just served with chips.

10 tomatillos, husks removed
2 serrano chiles, finely
  chopped, including seeds
1 clove garlic, minced
¼ cup chopped white onion

¼ cup chopped fresh cilantro
salt
water to thin mixture to
  desired consistency

Place tomatillos in a saucepan and cover with water. Simmer until tender, drain and cool. Combine ingredients. You may wish to chop using a food processor. Add salt to taste and enough water to thin to desired consistency. Serve at room temperature or cover and chill.

Makes 2½ cups

PICO DE GALLO

Pico de Gallo means "beak of the rooster" in Spanish. The "bits" of ingredients resemble the way the rooster pecks his food.

3 tomatoes, seeded and
  coarsely chopped
1 cup chopped white onion
1 can (4 oz.) chopped green
  chiles

⅓ cup chopped fresh cilantro
2 jalapeño chiles, seeded and
  minced
3 tbs. fresh lime juice
¾ tsp. salt

Combine all ingredients. Cover and chill.

Makes 2½ cups

SALSA CRUDA

*Salsa Cruda is an all-purpose salsa, similar to **Salsa Fresca** and others. Experiment with different combinations of ingredients to develop your own "signature" salsa.*

2 cups chopped fresh tomatoes
1 cup canned crushed
  tomatoes with added puree
¼ cup chopped yellow onion
2 green onions, thinly sliced
1 tbs. canned chopped
  jalapeño chiles

2 fresh serrano chiles, seeded
  and minced
2 tsp. fresh lime juice
¼ cup chopped fresh cilantro
¼ tsp. ground cumin
¼ tsp. crumbled dried oregano
¼ tsp. salt

Combine all ingredients. Cover and chill.

Makes 3 cups

SALSA PICANTE

To peel a tomato, immerse it in boiling water for several seconds. Make a slit in the skin with a sharp knife and it will slip off easily.

4 medium tomatoes, peeled and seeded
8 green onions, thinly sliced
5 pickled jalapeño chiles, minced

4 cloves garlic, minced
2 tbs. olive oil
¼ cup chopped fresh cilantro
½ tsp. salt

Coarsely chop all ingredients by hand or with a food processor. Cover and chill.

Makes 1½ cups

JICAMA SALSA

Jicama is a root vegetable from South America that is gaining in popularity throughout the country. Its crunchy texture is very appealing in this salsa. Try this with quesadillas.

½ lb. tomatillos, husks removed
½ lb. jicama, peeled
1 fresh jalapeño chile, seeded
  and finely minced

⅓ cup lime juice
½ tsp. salt
dash cayenne pepper

Remove cores from tomatillos. Chop tomatillos and jicama until fine. Add remaining ingredients and season to taste. Serve immediately or cover and refrigerate.

Makes 2 cups

TEQUILA SALSA

This quick and easy salsa is delicious with fajitas or chips. The serrano chiles are very hot, so adjust the amount if you wish.

1 can (28 oz.) tomatoes
3 serrano chiles, seeded and minced
½ cup chopped red onion
¼ cup tequila
grated zest (colored peel without white membrane) and
juice of 1 lime
¼ cup chopped fresh cilantro
1 tsp. salt
½ tsp. pepper

By hand or with a food processor, coarsely chop ingredients and combine. Cover and refrigerate.

Makes 3 cups

PICO DE GALLO WITH MEXICAN BEER

The Mexican beer adds interesting flavor, but tequila, vodka or regular beer would work as well. This is an all-purpose salsa that's good with chips or with tacos.

2 cups chopped fresh tomatoes
2 serrano chiles, seeded and finely chopped
¼ cup chopped sweet white onion
2 tbs. chopped fresh cilantro
¼ cup Mexican beer
1 tsp. sugar
1 tsp. salt
juice of 1 lime

Combine all ingredients and chill for 30 minutes.

Makes 2½ cups

INDEX

Notes

Notes

Notes

Notes

Notes

Notes

Notes

Notes